This book is dedicated to my mom and dad, who are my first loves and first teachers. Also, to my grandmothers: Thank you for the cherished memories.

To my husband: Thank you for your patience.

Ready, Set, Go
To
Grandma's

Sophia Carter-Parker, M.Ed., Ed.M.
Illustrated by Enigdesign

Hi! My name is Cooper but everybody calls me Coop.

I love going to my grandma's house!

Some people have to pack suitcases and take trains or planes to get to their grandma's house.

Others have to take long car rides to get to their grandma's house.

Not me, though!

My grandma doesn't live far away from my house.

Sometimes, we walk to grandma's house but most of the time, we take a short car ride to get to my grandma's house.

When I get to my grandma's house, she is always so happy to see me!
Grandma always smiles at me and says, "Awww, that's my baby."
Even though, I'm not a baby anymore, grandma says, I'll always be her baby.

Grandma usually kisses me a lot.

Grandma also likes to squeeze my cheeks.

Sometimes, grandma tickles me a lot too.

I laugh and laugh and laugh.

One time, grandma told me that she would always love me,
even if at times, I don't love myself.

I don't really know what all that means but I think it means she
loves me a whole lot.

Grandma always comes to my rescue!

Mommy and daddy get so mad at grandma, when she rescues me.

They tell grandma that she is letting me have my way and that she is spoiling me.

Grandma is a Sunday school teacher, at her church.

Sunday school is so much fun!

In Sunday school, we sing songs, color and read stories.

In one story, a boy named David used a slingshot to win a fight with a bully, who was a big giant, named Goliath!

I like that story because the boy wasn't scared of the bully.

Another time, in grandma's Sunday school class, we read about a big flood.

The people got on a big boat with two of all the animals.

Then grandma taught us a song, singing, " Two by two, on the Arky, Arky, two by two, on the Arky, Arky."

That song was funny!

In Sunday school, we also practice for holiday plays. But at my grandma's church, they call the holiday plays Christmas and Easter plays.

When it's time for us to do our performances, in front of all the Sunday school people, grandma makes sure that I have a haircut, a new suit and shiny shoes.

After the Easter play, we usually go over to the park and find colored eggs and we eat jellybeans and lots of chocolate candy.

At grandma's house, there is a "Good Thing Can."

Grandma has a special can that she puts all kinds of goodies in, like: cookies, candies, lollipops, and chocolates.

The chocolate chip cookies are my favorites. Yum!

Sometimes, my aunt Crystal is at my grandma's house, with my cousins Liam and Noah.

I have so much fun with my cousins, at my grandma's house!

But grandma always says we make too much noise.

My Aunt Crystal is kind-of strict! Grandma lets me get away with stuff.

Not my aunt Crystal, though.

Sometimes, my aunt rolls her eyes at me and says, "Boy, don't

play with me, I'm not your grandma!"

Once a month, we have a big family dinner at my grandma's house.

Then, it's really a lot of noise and everybody has fun!

When everybody leaves, grandma smiles and tells me that she saved some of her extra cheesy, mac and cheese, just for me!

I sure am sad when I leave grandma's house.

I always miss my grandma.

I can't wait until my next visit with grandma!

CPSIA information can be obtained
at www.ICGtesting.com
Printed in the USA
LVHW070516241020
669611LV00003B/62